Buddhism For Beginners

The Buddha's Four Noble Truths and the Path to Awakening

©2015

Diane Clarke

Table Of Contents

Introduction

Chapter 1 - Suffering

Chapter 2 – Origin

Chapter 3 – Cessation

Chapter 4 – The Path

Parting Thoughts

MY GIFT TO YOU:
Don't Forget To Get Your Free E-books.

Go To The Link Below To Receive My 101 Favourite Spiritual Quotes, From Buddha, HH The Dalai Lama, Eckhart Tolle And Many More.

Also Receive The Bonus Book Command Your Life: Secrets To Managing your Own Destiny All For Free.

These Books Are Just Small Gifts To Show My Gratitude For Buying My Book.

Visit www.eepurl.com/bnoryf
To Get Your Free Books Right Now.

Introduction

Buddhism is an ancient wisdom tradition, the name of which conjures up images of saffron-clad monks in distant monasteries. But although the Buddhist teachings are about 2,500 years old, they still speak to modern minds with a fresh relevance. That's because they are based on what the Buddha, Siddhartha Gautama, learned about the human mind through his own experience. Buddhism exerts a powerful draw on people even today because it contains timeless truths about human nature that the Buddha discovered by his own fearless exploration of mind and reality—and it carefully outlines a path that shows spiritual seekers how to discover these truths for themselves as a matter not of religious dogma, but of personal experience.

Siddhartha Gautama was a prince of an Indian clan, the Shakyas, of around the fifth or sixth century BC. Although he was raised to be a king and trained in the arts of warfare and statecraft, he became dissatisfied with his sheltered life in the palace. He was haunted by existential questions about how to live life most meaningfully, why we suffer and die, and what we can do about that. So he escaped the palace in the dead of night to become a wandering mendicant and spiritual seeker—what was, at the time, called a *shramana* or renunciate.

The Buddha's time was a very interesting one. It seemed

there were a number of such princes who could not shed their kingly inheritances fast enough. The *shramana* movement that the young Siddhartha joined was a thriving, diverse community of seekers and drop-outs who were not satisfied with traditional religious answers to life's great questions. They adopted a lifestyle of voluntary poverty and lived in the forests, or wandered from town to town begging for their daily bread. They spent their time meditating, performing austerities, and discussing spiritual matters; held a great diversity of opinion, debating every point; and were quite bold and ambitious in their explorations. They were the pioneers of India's ancient science of mind, and their ideas and techniques would later be developed and systematized as the philosophies, meditative practices, and yogas of Buddhism, Hinduism, and Jainism.

Siddhartha spent his time learning whatever he could from the highly regarded *shramana* teachers of his time and quickly reached the pinnacle of the meditations that they taught. But he still was not satisfied that he had come to a solution to the existential problem that vexed him. He tried extreme fasting and bodily mortification in order to loosen his attachment to the body, but that did not work either; he nearly died. Finally, he gave in and resumed eating. Then he sat beneath a pipal tree, which became known as the tree of *Bodhi* or enlightenment, and applied his attention, made powerful, stable, and precise through his mastery of meditation, to his body and mind, hoping to find ultimate insight into the human condition.

As he sat beneath the *Bodhi* tree, Siddartha was assailed by visions of a demon called Mara, who tried to deter him from reaching the consummation of his path. But Siddhartha was not put off the goal. He attained three knowledges: the knowledge of his past lives, the knowledge of the workings of cause and effect and how dependent arising produces our condition, and the knowledge that he had been released from samsara. Thus he became the Buddha, or Awakened One.

After the Buddha attained awakening under the *Bodhi* tree, the first place he visited was a deer park near Varanasi in India, where he met his former companions. His companions were fellow travelers on the spiritual path who, prior to the Buddha's enlightenment, had looked up to Siddhartha as a leader. But when Siddhartha gave up the extreme ascetic practices of self-starvation and denial of the body, they thought he had lost his nerve. They abandoned him.

Now he appeared before them as a *Buddha*. To communicate his spiritual realization to his former companions, the Buddha formulated the Dharma to which he had awakened as the four noble truths. He knew that he first had to get them to understand that the spiritual search is an answer to a problem. That problem is *suffering*. Suffering is not a random, senseless occurrence, but can be traced to an *origin*. Because suffering comes from a cause, there is a chance of something else—suffering could actually be ended. There is a real possibility of *cessation*, or *nirvana*. Lastly, the Buddha explained how to bring about that cessation by means of a *path*.

The entirety of the Buddha's teachings can be included in the framework of these four truths. As the Buddha himself began with the four noble truths when he turned the wheel of Dharma for the first time, we could not hope to improve upon his formula; it is fitting that we should introduce the Buddhist teachings in the same way.

Chapter 1 - Suffering

Suffering, as a noble truth, is this: Birth is suffering, aging is suffering, sickness is suffering, death is suffering, sorrow and lamentation, pain, grief and despair are suffering; association with the loathed is suffering, dissociation from the loved is suffering, not to get what one wants is suffering—in short, suffering is the five categories of clinging objects. — The Sutra of Turning the Wheel of Dharma

The Buddhist emphasis on suffering might seem pessimistic at first glance. Why, you may wonder, does Buddhism go on about miserable things, instead of focusing on the positive? It may be that the Buddha was a poor student of happiness. Perhaps if he had had the benefit of modern seminars, books, and techniques for becoming happier, he wouldn't have felt the inner disquiet that drove him from his comfortable palace life to seek wisdom in the wilderness.

But the Buddhist approach is not all doom and gloom. The Buddha did not recommend that we dwell on suffering so that we can get depressed. He believed that we need to make an honest confrontation with our own present mind, our own present situation, to get to know ourselves inside out. This means that we cannot gloss over the reality: we often feel dissatisfied, restless, stressed, confused, alone, anxious, bored. Buddhism says that we must start with a frank look at the truth.

In our modern society, we are constantly getting messages about the importance of happiness. We are told that we should be happy in our jobs, in our relationships, with our families—with our lives. Happiness is the meaning of life—that's obvious, right?

But do we actually benefit from this message? It seems the modern cult of happiness actually makes some people feel worse. They feel a distance between the ideal happy life we are all supposed to be living and the fact of their own dissatisfaction. Many people, when they first encounter the Buddhist teaching on suffering, feel a tremendous sense of relief. As soon as they get the news that they're allowed to acknowledge that they are not always happy, they begin to feel better. *Oh, thank goodness, it's normal!* The noble truth of suffering is easy to relate to because we all have suffered.

The word for "suffering" used in the scriptures is *duḥkha* in Sanskrit. This comes from the roots *du* and *kha*. *Du* means bad, *kha* means the hole at the hub of a wheel where the axle fits. *Duhkha* means that the axle-hole is badly made, the axle does not fit properly, or it is off-center. The result is a bumpy, unpleasant ride. The opposite of *duhkha*, *sukha* or "happiness," "pleasure," means that the hole has been drilled perfectly and the ride will be a smooth and enjoyable one.

The presence of suffering or *duhkha* tells us that something is not quite right, something is off. There are, broadly speaking, three kinds of suffering we can experience: *suffering of suffering, suffering of change,* and *suffering of being conditioned.*

The *suffering of suffering* is the most obvious kind. It can range from the commonplace hassles of life, such as the annoyance of having to wait at a bus stop in the cold or getting bitten to a mosquito, to more extreme kinds of suffering—the death of a family member, starvation, heartbreak, terminal illness. Buddhism does not discount ordinary irritations as too trivial to be considered suffering, but includes them because they share the common feature of the suffering of suffering: it's unpleasant when we experience them, and we are glad when they're over. So the Buddhist term *suffering* is not limited to such dramatic instances as injury, sickness, and extreme anguish, but includes everyday occurrences.

You can find the truth of this in your own experience. Look at your mind when you are waiting in a long line at the supermarket. Do you feel bored, restless, or annoyed? Do you look at the people in line in front of you, with huge carts full of groceries, and inwardly groan, imagining how long it will take for the cashier to finish ringing them up? Do you find yourself wishing the line would move faster and you could start driving home already? In such typical thoughts you can detect the presence of *duhkha*; there is the emotion of dissatisfaction, of wanting the situation to be other than what it is.

Suppose you finally escape the tedium of the supermarket check-out counter. You pack the groceries in the trunk of your car and sit down behind the steering wheel. You put on some of your favorite music and start driving home. But on the way, you hit bottleneck traffic. Again you're stuck, again bored, wondering what the holdup is. Is there construction ahead? An accident? You don't know. You just have to wait. On top of that, your A/C is giving off some weird smell. You wrinkle your nose. Another small irritation.

Buddhism does not call attention to these instances so that we can feel that life is one endless hassle, but so that we can begin to understand what goes on in our minds when we're faced with unwanted situations. Somehow the approach of closing our eyes and pretending that irritating things don't irritate us just doesn't work. We have to actually start where we are, with our own dissatisfied minds. Otherwise, as soon as we encounter a more serious kind of suffering, we will get knocked off our seat and our butt will hit the ground hard. It is better to start with our butt on the ground from the beginning. Then we are in contact with the reality of our ground, and we do not get caught up in a spiritual fantasy.

* * *

One of the keystone statements of the Buddhism is: *All conditioned phenomena are impermanent.* What does that mean? A *conditioned* phenomenon is anything that has come about due to causes and conditions. That covers a wide range of things, from all inanimate, material objects to all animals and people. It also includes all of our thoughts, feelings, sensations, habits—anything whatsoever that partakes of the life of the mind. If it came into existence, it did so in dependence on causes and conditions. Buddhism calls this truth *dependent arising.*

If a phenomenon is conditioned—that is to say, if it came into being in dependence on causes and conditions—it is impermanent. It will not last forever. And though it may persist for a while, it will be subject to change and decay. Some things last longer than others. Vegetables spoil pretty quickly; mountains have a longer lifespan. But a mountain never stays that same, not even for a moment. It is constantly altered by the erosions of wind and water; over long millennia, they soften its shape. Plants and trees change its surface. Earthquakes cause huge portions of it to crumble and fall.

The device on which you're reading this book is subject to

the same wear and tear. When you first bought it, it was flawless. But maybe now it has a dent in the corner or a scratch on the screen. One day it will give up the ghost, and you will have to replace it.

People, likewise, are impermanent. We are all uncomfortably aware of our mortality. We are beings composed of parts: our bodies are made up of bones, blood vessels, and organs that are in turn made of cells; combined with our minds, they make up a person. The cells in our body are constantly dying and being replaced by new ones. Once you start meditating, you notice that the mind, too, has little stability; it is constantly changing, subject to an endlessly shifting stream of thoughts. The entire world is like a great river, in ceaseless motion. Whatever arises will also cease to be.

The second kind of suffering is the *suffering of change*. When we meet with happy conditions in our lives, they may stay that way for a long or short time, but not forever. Eventually, they will meet with impermanence. A happy relationship may end when a partner leaves us. We may have a good, stable job, only to lose our income when we are unexpectedly laid off. Or the scoop of ice cream we were enjoying may suddenly fall out of the cone onto the pavement. When a happy state gives way to suffering, that is the suffering of change.

When you gradually come to accept the reality of

impermanence, that all meeting ends in parting, you come into contact with reality. The acceptance of things as they are allows for you to find a sense of peace and clarity amidst the flux. It becomes a source of strength, as you realize that contentment is not to be found in attachment to the shifting circumstances of life, but in cultivating a calm equanimity and bravery that will carry you through both good and bad times.

* * *

Subtler is the anxiety that we have that the good things in our lives could be undone by some misfortune. Take that happy relationship from earlier. Although everything is going well, we may sometimes have doubts and worries about what will happen if the relationship turns sour or our partner is cheating on us. We often have some feeling of insecurity in the background. At the threshold of awareness there is a nagging sense that even our present happiness will not last forever. The background anxiety about impermanence is part of the *suffering of being conditioned.*

The suffering of being conditioned is a very subtle level of suffering. It exists because we are conditioned, finite beings. We are not plugged into this world the way a television set plugs into a wall, so that the world's currents flow through us and we pick up its signals. If that were so, we could simply unplug. We could turn ourselves off. But we are part of the world; we are products of the give and take between us and the world. We cannot simply extricate ourselves from the situation.

The unease we feel at being part of the flux, part of the ebb and flow of causes and conditions, is present as the background of our experience. That is why it is also called *pervasive*. This background of subtle suffering creates the general atmosphere of hope and fear that informs many of our thoughts and deeds.

The recognition of the reality of suffering in your own mind takes tremendous bravery and self-honesty. It need not be an occasion for falling into depression or despair, but could be accompanied by transcendental good cheer. By examining suffering, your are actually getting to the bottom of it. You could actually rejoice that you have the guts to unravel suffering's mystery instead of covering it up. The truth of suffering is called a *noble* truth because its recognition ennobles you. It is the foundational insight that makes it possible to walk the spiritual path. That unflinching strength of vision could be an inspiration to make further self-discoveries.

Chapter 2 - Origin

The origin of suffering, as a noble truth, is this: It is the craving that produces renewal of being accompanied by enjoyment and lust, and enjoying this and that; in other words, craving for sensual desires, craving for being, craving for non-being.

The second noble truth is the origin of suffering. Suffering, like everything else conditioned, comes about from a cause. *Something* causes suffering to come into being. It does not just come from nowhere.

One of the most profound discoveries the Buddha made is that suffering is not like some random projectile that is hurled at us from the chaos of the world, not "the slings and arrows of outrageous fortune," but that it is manufactured in our own minds. It is a domestic problem. We can't put the blame someone else.

Go back to the original meaning of *duḥkha*, the poorly made wheel. Because we did not drill the hole into the wheel properly, the axle doesn't fit, and every bump in the road becomes a savage jolt. Even level pavement doesn't yield a smooth ride. We can't remake the road, we can't ask the world to change for our sake, so we have to start with mending the cart. That means working on our own mind through the practice of meditation.

Suffering comes from passion, aggression, and confusion, called the *kleshas* or neuroses, which in turn are based on fundamental ignorance. Ignorance, or *avidya*, is fundamentally misapprehending the nature of things. Our perception is out of alignment with the truth, and this generates a host of problems. The fact is that we ourselves and the world are in flux, never staying stable for even a moment. Ignorance is an attempt to freeze that flux into something solid and stable. We would like to freeze one part and call it "self," "I," "me," the other part we try to freeze and call "other." We attempt to impose some order on the basic of impermanent state of things by diktat so that we can have solid ground to stand on and a little island of security called "me" "mine" in the midst of change and uncertainty.

This is a mistake—the original mistake—but once we've made it, it triggers a self-sustaining process, a feedback loop that just keeps going and producing more confusion and suffering. This feedback loop Buddhism calls *samsara*. The truth is that there is no "I" or "me" to hold on to. What we are is just aggregates of physical and mental events-- the heaps or *skandhas*. The problem comes when we grasp onto these aggregates as "me" or "mine."

The Buddha likened the aggregates to a dog tied by a leash to a post. The dog cannot really go anywhere, but if he moves, he moves around the post. If he lies down, he lies down next to the post. The post becomes, for the dog, an utterly familiar item; it becomes *his* post, and even though it limits him, he identifies with it and feels comfort in his restriction.

Likewise, even though the aggregates limit and restrict us, we identify with them. We are stuck in our crummy, shabby little apartment, surrounded by our own mess, but it is *our* apartment. We would like to protect it and return to it after a long day at work. We feel relief when we smell its familiar smell of long habitation. We never notice that the air has become stale and the clutter claustrophobic.

The aggregates are five in number: form, feeling, perception, conditioning, and consciousness. *Form* is the level of the body. It is embodied experience, the sensory level of experiencing oneself as a being of flesh and blood, with arms and legs, eyes, ears, a sense of smell, and so on.

Feeling corresponds to what psychologists call "valence." When the eye comes into contact with a visual form, or the ear comes into contact with a sound, we experience it as pleasant, unpleasant, or neutral. That positive, negative, or neutral quality of any given experience is called feeling in Buddhism.

On the basis of feeling, *perception* picks out the distinctive qualities of the felt object and relates them to previous experience. At this level, we identify the contents of our experience by relating them to memory and previously formed concepts. Then we form an emotional attitude to the object: passion for positive objects, aggression towards negative objects, and indifference to neutral ones.

Passion is the compulsion to draw pleasant things towards us, to possess them and identify with them in order to augment our sense of self. Aggression is a defensive attitude. We want to drive unpleasant things away from us, or throw up a shield so that they cannot get to us. Anything that we feel to be a threat to our survival, comfort, or sense of self becomes the target of our aggression. Indifference is related to confusion and ignorance. The object is neutral, irrelevant to our sense of self. So we adopt an attitude of not caring about it; we simply ignore it, which is a kind of stupidity because we refuse to be aware of anything in our experience that can't be used to reinforce the structure of ego.

Conditioning adds a further level of complexity to the picture. This is the level of mental dispositions and habits. It is *conditioning* in the sense that our dispositions are conditioned by experience, volitions, and actions from the past, and also in the sense that it conditions further volitions and therefore causes us to act (*karma*), which drives the engine of samsara—that feedback loop or self-sustaining process in which suffering and confusion perpetuate themselves.

The fifth and final aggregate, *consciousness*, represents the pinnacle of the ego's achievement. It is the level with which we are all most familiar. At this level there is an endless train of discursive thoughts and varied, irregular emotions. There is always something going on. Consciousness is hyperactive, never wanting to allow a gap to form in the middle of the endless procession of thoughts and emotions. It coordinates all the other processes and incorporates them into the central narrative of the ego: the "I" as an agent in the world, where good and bad things happen to "me," where "I" experience triumphs and defeats. It is at this level that we are aware of our "self" as the main protagonist in our own story in which we have ups and downs, go through trials, work hard, fall in love, and so on. Consciousness relates every aspect of our experience to our story and forms the vision of ourselves as an independent, continuously existing, unitary self.

It is okay if you do not understand the idea of the five aggregates completely at first. We are meant to examine our own aggregates in meditation and relate them to our experience. Through meditation, the meaning of these ideas will become clear. Once we have worked our attention into something very steady and precise through the practices of calm-abiding and mindfulness meditation, we can turn that attention towards form, feeling, perception, conditioning, and consciousness. Examining each of the aggregates in turn, we look for the presence of the self or *atman*. Is there anything in form that is permanent, independently existing, singular and lasting? Is there anything—a self—that is "I," "me," "myself," or "mine?" If not, can this self be found in feeling, perception, conditioning, or consciousness?

We find that our aggregates only have the illusion of continuity, that when we look at them closely, we only see a series of momentary flashes of events. It is as if we were watching a film in the theater, and the film slowed down enough that we could see each of the individual frames. The illusion that we were actually watching people and things move around on the screen is totally shattered. We can see the gaps between the frames and are shaken out of our suspension of disbelief into an acute awareness that the images we see are just the light of the projector shining through a roll of film onto a surface.

As we analyze our "self" into their constituent elements, it becomes clear that its unity and continuity is just as illusory as the film. Investigating each of the aggregates in turn, we find that none of them is really a good candidate for being the identity of "me." What about outside the aggregates, then? Can the self, the "I" be something other than the five aggregates? But we never observe this other thing. The five aggregates are an exhaustive list of all mental and physical experience. If the self is something other then the aggregates, it is not anything we can experience. How, then, could it be what "I" am?

The non-existence of the self is the liberating insight of the Buddhist Dharma. The word for this non-existence of self in Sanskrit is *anatman* or selflessness, from *an-* meaning "not" and *atman*, "self." If the origin of suffering is ignorance, the compulsion to freeze and solidify the free flow of experience into self and other, then the solution to the problem of suffering is to cultivate a direct, experiential insight into *anatman*.

* * *

According to the Buddha, the fundamental ignorance of grasping at the existence of self is a problem that we cannot trace to its beginning, and therefore we cannot trace the feedback loop of *samsara* to its beginning. We do not know when the whole thing started, or if it in fact *ever* started. As far as we know, we've been making the same mistake since time without beginning. Once the process is in motion, it just keeps itself going endlessly.

There are twelve stages in the process, and they span multiple lifetimes: past lives stretching back in time to we know not when, and future lives that will continue until we break the cycle. The first stage is ignorance, the tendency to freeze the changing continuity of experience into solid blocks, to create a comfortable island of "I" so that the flux of momentary events does not freak us out. The traditional image of this stage in Tibetan art is of a blind old woman, feeling her way around in the dark with a walking stick. Ignorance does not relate with the world and the mind directly, but by the medium of self-grasping, by its frozen concepts.

Because of ignorance, *conditioning* or *formation* comes into being. The effect of ignorance is to condition our mind to have certain dispositions to act. The word for action is *karma*. Here *karma* does not refer to an impersonal cosmic law that punishes evildoers and rewards the good guys. It just means action, which is part of the natural order of cause and effect. Our actions lead to consequences and color our mental life. We each have different tendencies and personalities because of the actions we have undertaken in the past. So karma further modifies the mind's conditioning and often leads to unexpected consequences. The image of conditioning is a potter working with clay. We are making something, we are conditioning our minds somehow, but because of the blindness of the previous stage, we are not quite sure what we are throwing on the potter's wheel.

The next stage is *consciousness*. In this case, we are specifically talking about the projecting consciousness which will project us towards our next rebirth and keep the samsaric process going. Based on the karmic conditioning from the previous life, a consciousness is formed that will be the basis of the next life. Consciousness is represented by the image of a monkey in a tree. Just as a monkey swings from tree to tree, consciousness goes from life to life. The excitable, distractible nature of the monkey is also a perfect simile for our ordinary discursive consciousness, which is constantly jumping from thought to thought and hardly rests on a single point for very long.

Consciousness gives rise to *namarupa* or *name-and-form*—that is to say, the sum of mental and physical parts that we call an individual person. We are at the stage of a baby in the womb. This is an abbreviation of the five aggregates: *form* is just form, while *name* stands for the mental aggregates of feeling, perception, conditioning, and consciousness. Here "consciousness" and "conditioning" mean the aggregates we discussed earlier, rather than the previous two stages just mentioned. The image is of a person in a boat at sea. The person is our mind, while the boat is the body in which we navigate the ocean of being.

The next stage is the *six senses*. The baby in the womb develops eyes, ears, a nose, a tongue, and nerves under the surface of the skin. In addition, there is also a sixth sense faculty, the mind, that will pick up information from the other five senses and sense another kind of object: thoughts and other such mental phenomena. This is represented by the image of a house with five windows and a door. The house is empty because the child is not yet out in the world, but the basic setup is there—the windows and door through which the child will interact with its environment.

Once the child is born, the senses come into *contact* with sense objects. Contact is the sixth stage. It is represented by a man and woman making love beneath a blanket. Just like human sexual union, the joining of senses with sense objects is productive because it gives rise to further conscious experience.

Contact produces *feeling*. Whatever comes to touch our senses is experienced as painful, pleasurable, or neutral. This is represented by the rather vivid image of an arrow piercing a person's eye. Our vision does not simply give us an objective window through which to view the world; the world pierces us all the time with pain and pleasure. Like an arrow in the eye, it cannot be ignored.

Because of feeling, we experience *craving*. The Sanskrit word for craving is *trishna*, which literally means "thirst." We crave and thirst after pleasurable feelings, and when painful feelings assail us, we crave and thirst for them to end. Thirst is experienced as suffering, which is why the Buddha said that the origin of suffering is "craving for sensual desires, craving for being, craving for non-being." We thirst after water so that the water will quench our thirst. The logic is very circular. What we want is not the object of our desire; we want to end our wanting. We know this because, once we get what we desire, we do not remain satisfied for long. We begin to crave something else. We are always thirsty. The image of thirst is a woman pouring tea for a man. He thirsts for tea, but after the tea he will thirst for something else.

Because we crave something, we reach for it and try to take it. This is *grasping,* the eighth stage. Craving was an emotion, a drive, but grasping is an active movement towards the object. The Sanskrit word is *upadana*, literally "fuel." Fire clings to and burns up a piece of wood, then spreads to another piece of wood, just as we cling to and use up the sense objects, then move on to the next. The image of grasping is a man reaching to pluck fruit from a tree. We are actively moving to take what we desire.

It is here that there is a possibility to break the chain reaction. Through meditation, we are able to watch the process of our own feeling, craving, and grasping happening all the time. As our mind slows down, a gap may open up between craving and grasping. First we crave something—an ice cream, perhaps—then instinctively we move towards it. But if we can slow our mental speed, then between the craving and the grasping a space opens up, and we can simply let go of the craving. We can choose to disrupt the machinery of samsara, which causes the process to slow down. This introduces a radical possibility: we could actually bring the whole process of suffering to a halt.

But ordinarily, we do not open up a gap between craving and grasping. Grasping causes new karmic conditioning to form, called *becoming*. The conditioning of the second stage referred to an inheritance from the past. It was something that had already formed. At the stage of *becoming*, we are talking about new conditioning that will become the basis for future lives. Now we can see how the volitional process—craving, grasping, then becoming—gives rise to new karmic dispositions. As was mentioned earlier, the Buddhist idea of karma is not of a cosmic system of justice, but the operation of cause and effect within the psychology of the individual. It is a natural process.

The image of becoming is a bride before her wedding. Something is already in motion, but it has not yet been completed. Still, a point of no return has been reached. It is too late for the bride to back out. She is already in her bridal clothes and will have to go through with the wedding, for better or for worse.

Because of the becoming of new karmic conditioning, the process of samsara will continue. The individual's consciousness will take a new *birth*. There are, in Buddhism, six realms or kinds of birth we can take. For example, we could become a human or an animal. Which kind of birth we take will depend on the our actions or karma and the conditioning they create. A human birth is the most desirable from a Buddhist perspective, because it affords the best opportunity to practice the spiritual path and get free from the vicious cycle.

Because we are born, we must sooner or later die. That is the brute fact of impermanence. Between birth and death there is aging. So the twelfth and last stage of dependent arising is called *aging and death*. The end result of the original ignorance is that we must go through birth, aging, sickness, and death again and again for as long as we remain in our ignorance. The traditional image is of pallbearers carrying a corpse to the cremation ground.

Western culture shies away from considering our mortality, but if we acknowledge this harsh reality, we put our whole lives in perspective. With mindfulness of our own impermanence, of the fact that we are going to die, we will not waste our time in this life but make the most of it. The teachings say that in this life we have a *precious human body*, which is precious not just because of being human, but because certain other conditions, such as the fact that we feel an inclination to practice the spiritual path and that someone has already come and explained how to do it from A to Z. Not only can we take advantage of this received wisdom, but there are many others who have already done so. They have realized within themselves the meaning of the teachings, in full or in part, so that we can rely on them for guidance and instruction. We have these advantages because we were born in a human body in this place at this time. When we reflect on our limited time with this life, we will give birth to a strong motivation to put our advantages to good use.

Chapter 3 - Cessation

Cessation of suffering, as a noble truth, is this: It is remainderless fading and ceasing, giving up, relinquishing, letting go and rejecting, of that same craving.

The cessation of suffering is liberation or release (*moksha*), also known as *nirvana*. It is easy to relate to the concept of nirvana as a Buddhist version of heaven—some distant religious promise. That kind of nirvana is a mere fantasy, the logical counterpart to samsara. But the Buddha proclaimed the third noble truth, the cessation of suffering, as a real possibility. He made an outrageous declaration of amnesty for all sentient beings—prisoners of samsara. For him, nirvana was not just an abstract religious concept, but the waking reality which he discovered. It was the very personal, very real experience of freedom to which he awoke under the Bodhi tree.

While samsara is the feedback loop we get stuck in, in which ignorance and craving beget more confused situations, which beget further ignorance and craving, then nirvana is what's left after that loop is ended. It is the freedom that we have when the vicious cycle is over. We could begin to get a taste of that freedom right now, by opening up a gap in our discursive thought through the practice of meditation.

It is as if we have always been suffering from a fever, so that we don't even know what it is like to be well. Because we have no basis for comparison, it is very hard for us to imagine getting cured of our fever. We doubt that it's even possible; we may even doubt that we are sick at all. But, through the advice of someone else, we decide to try a new medicine. Because we haven't ever been well, we can't really understand what the medicine is for. Still, we try it, and our fever temporarily stops. We feel extremely soothed and cooled, and we realize that we had always been overheated, sick, and out of sorts. This opens up the possibility that we could cure our sickness altogether.

Nirvana means "extinguished," "blown out," as of a fire. After the flames of neurosis—of passion, aggression, and confusion—have been put out, what remains is the profound coolness and peace of nirvana. To attain nirvana, you have to walk the spiritual path. There is no shortcut, but you have to work on your mind and slowly take apart the machinery of ego-grasping, which is the engine of samsara.

Still, you can get a foretaste of cessation from the practice of meditation. Nirvana is connected to what the Buddha called *luminous mind*. The basic nature of the mind has a natural radiance that has always been there. In meditation, we are sometimes able to glimpse this luminous mind through a gap in the murk of ignorance and neurosis. But it is usually covered up. In the *Pabhassara Sutta* or discourse on luminosity, the Buddha states, "Luminous, monks, is the mind, and it is defiled by incoming defilements."

This luminous mind is featureless, the ground of being, our unconditioned basic nature. It is pure, naked knowing, without object. In the same discourse, the Buddha says that we must have some experience of the luminous mind in order to develop our minds on the path of meditation. So we can see that having a glimpse or foretaste of nirvana is a necessary step on the path. It makes the path workable; it takes the possibility of nirvana from the realm of our religious imagination into the intimate domain of personal experience.

Luminosity refers to the mind's intrinsic purity from defilements. It is primordial; it never came into being and so cannot cease to be. Although neuroses and self-grasping appear to becloud the mind, in reality they cannot touch the basic purity of awareness. Likewise, clouds may cover up the sun, but behind the clouds the sun still shines. Like luminous mind, nirvana is also not a conditioned phenomenon; as it is the result of removing the causes and conditions of samsara, it is permanent. Once nirvana is attained, suffering will not return.

Here you might have some doubts. There is a semantic problem with using the word "suffering" as a translation of *duhkha*. "Suffering" suggests that we are the passive recipients of some pain from outside, while *duhkha* denotes that the axle-hole of a wheel is off-center or badly drilled. The concept of *duhkha* suggests that something is throwing us off, and that we ourselves are the authors of our misfortune because we have done a bad job handling our minds. We have screwed up something at a fundamental level and now a chain reaction has compounded the the bad result into a big mess. So we need a basic reeducation about what suffering is and what it is to be free of suffering.

The cessation of suffering does not mean that, if someone pricks you with a pin, it will not hurt. It doesn't work like that. What cessation means is that a pin-prick will not set off the usual chain reaction in your mind. Because you have dismantled the whole structure of ego or self-grasping, there is no sense that you have to defend yourself from threats or gather up pleasures and comforts. The need to prove your own existence through the self-deceptions of ego has vanished without a trace. That is what it means to speak of the "cessation of suffering."

The person who has achieved this cessation, this nirvana, is called an *arhat*. An arhat is someone who has fully realized the reality of egolessness. She has understood, through direct experience and not mere intellect, that there is no self to be found anywhere; the reflex of self-grasping no longer operates anywhere in her mind. For her, the dense fog of error has been totally dispersed by the rays of the morning sun of enlightenment, which, fully risen, illuminates her world completely.

> *Where neither water nor yet earth*
> *Nor fire nor air gain a foothold,*
> *There gleam no stars, no sun sheds light,*
> *There shines no moon, yet there no darkness reigns.*
>
> *When a sage, a brahman, has come to know this*
> *For himself through his own wisdom,*
> *Then he is freed from form and formless,*
> *Freed from pleasure and from pain.*
> — Bahiya Sutta

Chapter 4 – The Path

The way leading to cessation of suffering, as a noble truth, is this: It is simply the noble eightfold path, that is to say, right view, right intention; right speech, right action, right livelihood; right effort, right mindfulness, right concentration.

Having diagnosed the disease, explained its underlying cause, and spoken of the possibility of a cure, the Buddha prescribed a treatment plan, the noble eightfold path. The eightfold path is not quite eight stages that progress in a sequence, but can be likened to eight spokes of a wheel. The idea is that all eight spokes must be present to ensure the integrity of the wheel.

In this analogy, the wheel itself is the Dharma as it is practiced; it is our application of Dharma on the path. The Dharma is fundamentally something that must be put into practice, not just learned. Through practice, the wheel of Dharma makes contact with the ground and can move along the path. It is a very realistic approach. Spiritual practice, properly done, never takes off and flies into the air, but always stays planted on solid ground. We must be practical people and put in the hard work to make spiritual progress.

The eight limbs of the path can be grouped into three broad sections, or three trainings, called *view, conduct,* and *meditation*—or, alternately, *wisdom, ethics,* and *samadhi* or meditative concentration. In order to start walking the path we must first have some sense of the view, and then we can train in ethical conduct, which prepares our mind for more profound meditation practice. That, in turn, allows us to go more deeply into the view. In that way we progress by the cyclical turning of the wheel.

The training in wisdom consists of *right view* and *right intention.* Right view means to see things as they are in reality. It is not so much about seeing the world through fixed opinions, through a set of theoretical constructs, but about taking a very realistic view. In the beginning, right view does rely on theoretical ideas, but not in a heavy-handed, overly scholastic way; instead, you learn how to analyze and understand your present situation. Right view is sensitive and attentive to reality as it unfolds in your own experience.

Right view involves an understanding of karma. Part of the picture of our suffering is that we are afflicted with confusion about what to do. We keep performing the same actions without noticing that they lead to bad consequences, and we mostly shun the actions that will bring about positive results. We call this "confusion," *moha,* but we could just as easily translate it as "stupidity" because it is an insensitive refusal to stomach the truth about our behavior.

With right view, we see things as they are: we know that good karmas lead to good results, and bad karmas lead to bad results. It may sound simplistic, but actually it is very subtle. For example, if we haven't got much to wear, we may find stealing clothes to be convenient for our material needs, but do we consider the distorting effect it will have on our mind? The act of stealing leaves an imprint somewhere on consciousness; it conditions the mind in a certain way. With repetition, the distortion becomes extreme. Sooner or later, this deed will come to a bad result.

So right view involves knowing the difference between wholesome and unwholesome actions. It also involves a realistic understanding of the nature of things. We understand that anything that comes into existence will also cease to be; because it is conditioned, it is impermanent. We understand that these impermanent things cannot be relied on to give us any lasting satisfaction; they are part of the total picture of suffering. And we understand that there is no permanent, lasting, singular self or ego to be found anywhere in our experience, that the so-called "I" is just a belief produced by bad mental habits. We have, furthermore, an understanding of the four noble truths.

Right view informs *right intention*. If we understand the

difference between wholesome and unwholesome actions, then we are motivated to give up the unwholesome behaviors and adopt wholesome ones. With an understanding of how futile it is to struggle for worldly satisfactions, we will want to give those up, too, and exert ourselves on the spiritual path. We will understand the harmful effects of malice and wish to cultivate kindness within hearts and harmless behavior towards others. Our conduct will be free from violence and our minds free from ill will.

* * *

The training of ethics divides into *right speech*, *right conduct*, and *right livelihood*. The basic principle of Buddhist ethics is *ahimsa*, non-violence or non-harm. We strive to avoid behaviors that harm ourselves and others and to rid ourselves of harmful tendencies.

Right speech refers to avoiding lying, slander or divisive speech, verbal abuse and harshness, and meaningless chatter, instead favoring truthful, unitive, gentle, and meaningful words. As it says in the *Abhaya Sutta*, "In the case of words that the Tathagata (i.e., the Buddha) knows to be factual, true, beneficial, and endearing and agreeable to others, he has a sense of the proper time for saying them. Why is that? Because the Tathagata has sympathy for living beings."

Humans are linguistic creatures, and much of the good and bad we do, we do by opening our mouths to speak. Right speech is about using words in a manner that is beneficial rather than destructive and harmful. It's about cultivating sensitivity to the power of our words for good and ill.

Right conduct refers to the avoidance of bodily actions that harm others. This means avoiding killing, stealing, and sexual misconduct. The prohibition of killing includes both humans and animals, and we can take it in a broader sense to include any infliction of injury or bodily harm. The taking of life has severe moral consequences for the perpetrator and is extremely damaging to a person's psychological health. Soldiers who have committed atrocities on the battlefield, for example, often are tormented by post-traumatic stress disorder. Buddhism states that the consequence of killing out of aggression is hell. Hell can be thought of as a state of mind in which one is consumed by the fire of one's own hatred. The mind's own aggression and hatred turn inward upon itself. In contrast, one should protect life wherever and whenever possible. Even saving the lives of tiny insects is an act of tremendous compassion and merit.

Stealing is to take what is not given. The harmful effects of stealing are well known to anyone who has ever been the victim of a burglary; it places the burden of sudden financial hardship upon the victim. Systematic theft can harm an entire society; in our own time, we are well acquainted with the enormous economic strain that white-collar crime has caused for the general public. Stealing is usually motivated by greed. But ill-gotten gains seldom reward the greedy for very long; such people find that they never have enough. They are afflicted by a mentality of poverty. Wealth acquired honestly proves more stable, and generous people feel that they have enough to give freely.

Sexual misconduct refers to harmful sexual behavior. This could be anything from the severity of rape and sexual violence to infidelity, which wreaks havoc on relationships and is the source of heartbreak and grief. In Buddhism, sexual misconduct also includes having sexual relationships with those who have taken the vows of a monk or a nun, which destroys their vows and derails their spiritual progress. Those who engage in sexual misbehavior have a hard time finding joy in stable, lasting relationships; they may end up lonely or stuck with a quarrelsome partner. The Buddha understood that the misdirected libido could be a powerfully harmful force and admonished laypeople to maintain sexual behavior with consideration for the wellbeing of others rather than concern only with their own gratification.

Right livelihood is about how we earn a living. In work, as in conduct and speech, the gold standard of Buddhist ethics is *ahimsa*, non-harm. Work cannot be separated from spirituality. The work we do must agree with our spiritual and ethical principles. The *Vanijja Sutta* lists five kinds of work that a Buddhist layperson must not engage in. These are trading in weapons, trading in human beings (including slave trading, human trafficking, and prostitution), the meat business (such as slaughtering animals or raising them for slaughter), dealing in intoxicants and alcohol, and dealing in poisonous substances such as chemicals that harm living things. But wrong livelihood need not limited to just these five; it includes any kind of work that harms people or living beings.

* * *

If we have prepared ourselves by training in ethics, then we are ready to take up the training of meditation. We have carefully weeded out the verbal and physical behaviors that would impede our ability to progress in meditation, and we earn our living through honest work that brings benefit and value, rather than harm, to others. We are now ready for meditation, the mainstay of the Buddhist path.

These days, many beginning Buddhists start off straightaway with meditation. That is certainly a good thing, but Buddhist meditation belongs within the overall context of the view and ethics. If these are neglected, there is a danger that meditation could just be a form of relaxing or blissing out. It could lose touch with any sense of reality and just become a way of entertaining yourself with fantasies and self-deception.

Meditation is not about just relaxing and relieving stress. If that were the goal, no one would need to practice Buddhism. It would be enough to make a visit to the massage parlor or sip herbal tea and take holistic medicine. Meditation is fundamentally about working with your own present mind. You may want to improve yourself, enhance your cognitive abilities, get rid of your anxiety and depression, and so on, but those aims are not directly related to the practice of meditation. In order to bring an end to *duhkha*, you must start where you are, with your own mind in your own current situation, with all your problems, hangups, doubts, confusions, thoughts, and emotions.

Meditation means getting some familiarity with yourself. Most people have not actually bothered to get to know themselves. They avoid spending any time alone with their own minds, instead preferring to involve themselves in activities and entertainments of all sorts. But in the practice of meditation you do the very thing you have been avoiding; you spend time alone with your mind, slowly getting to know it and making friends with yourself. Through the practice of meditation, you learn to have kindness and compassion for yourself.

To meditate, you should have a proper place to sit. Purchasing a meditation cushion is a good idea. The cushion allows you to be a bit elevated from the ground, even as your knees touch the floor. The downward-sloping angle of your legs will help keep your back straight while you sit.

A straight back is a key point of meditation practice. Imagine that your spine is a stack of coins. If it leans too far forward or back, or to one side, the stack will come falling down. So keep your back straight and upright, but relaxed. There shouldn't be any tension in the posture.

You may cross your legs in the lotus position if you are able to do so without strain. Otherwise, you may put one foot on top of the opposite thigh—the half lotus—or both calves touching the floor, one in front of the other. Either way, it is ideal if your knees touch the floor. That will give stability to your posture.

Keep your hands folded in your lap, the fingers of your right hand resting upon the fingers of your left, with both thumbs touching gently. This is called the *mudra* or gesture of meditation.

Do not slouch your shoulders, but hold them back, like a vulture's wings. The elbows likewise should be held slightly apart from your body.

Your eyes should be open, gazing with relaxed focus at the space a few feet in front of you and below eye level. The tongue gently touches the roof of the mouth.

The posture of meditation is simple and earth-bound; it expresses your willingness to work with your mind practically. We do not shut out the world by closing our eyes, but leave them open. The reason is that we are in samsara and must accept it. We must be willing to face our situation as it is.

Meditation begins with mindfulness of the breath. The breath is a physical object, but it is subtle. We cannot see it, but only feel it. Still, breathing is a vital function. We have to breathe to live. So the breath is a very natural, very wholesome object of meditation, while still being somewhat abstract, like the mind.

You want to attend to the feeling of the breath as it goes in and out. To begin with, you could count the number of breaths from one to ten, then start over again. This makes it easier in the beginning to keep track of when your attention is on the breath and when you are distracted. Later, counting the breath may seem too heavy-handed. Then just place your attention gently on the breath. You may even find it is helpful to follow the breath as it goes out and dissolves into space, and then, during the in-breath, simply allow your mind to rest without an object.

When the mind wanders from the breath, it is not regarded as a problem. Simply label the distracting thoughts "Thinking" and return your attention to the breath. The mind will constantly wander in this way. When distractions happen, they are never good or bad, virtuous or sinful. They are simply distractions; you do not need to add an extra layer of judgment to your thoughts. Nothing has gone wrong with your meditation, but the mind's natural energy has caused it to move. Simply return to the breath. With time, it will be easier to catch deviations and your attention will be less likely to go astray.

Through meditation on the breath, the mind's speed, the rate at which it produces discursive thought, will slow down, and you will begin to feel an expanded sense of clarity, space, and peace. The mind is like a pond. If it is disturbed, it will be dark and murky. But let it be and the mud will slowly settle to the bottom. The waters will become still and transparent. Although we tend to want fast results, this happens so gradually that we do not even notice the change. Still, after a year or two of meditation, our friends may remark, "What happened to you? You're so calm and peaceful, like a different person!"

The peace of mind cultivated in mindfulness of the breath is called *shamatha* or calm abiding. Shamatha makes the mind clear and workable. Through shamatha, we develop a stable, refined attention that we can apply to any object. Thus shamatha is a prerequisite for the second kind of meditation, *vipashyana* or insight. In vipashyana, we use the powerful and stable attention cultivated in shamatha to examine the various aspects of our experience. We examine the five aggregates and note the presence of suffering. We see how momentary, impermanent events are constantly going on in our body and mind. We look for a continuous, singular self within the aggregates and find that no such thing can be found in the stream of constant change. Gradually our understanding of suffering, impermanence, and non-self deepens until it becomes realization.

The training in meditation is divided into *right effort*, *right mindfulness*, and *right samadhi*. Right effort is the application of our minds to the path. There should be some sort of joy involved; if we force ourselves, effort becomes a chore. Right effort strives to prevent and abandon *unwholesome* speech and action, as well as give rise to and maintain wholesome speech and action.

Right mindfulness is the steady placing of attention one-pointedly on the object of meditation. The quality of this attention is somewhat detached, but not wholly indifferent. Mindfulness has a sense of alertness and curiosity as it observes what is happening in the present moment. It is not concerned with laying a theoretical interpretation on things or judging them as good or bad, but simply watches what is going on. If you would like to learn more about mindfulness please purchase my book, Mindfulness: The Beginners Guide to Living in The Moment to Achieve Less Stress, More Happiness & Inner Peace inside it there are some great mindfulness techniques that can be practiced any time any place.

Finally, *right samadhi* or *right concentration* is the progressive deepening of meditative absorption. Here the meditator progresses through a series of meditative states called *jhanas* in Pali. These states are ever subtler and deeper levels of concentration. They are experiential stages that advanced meditators go through as they refine their attentional capacities more and more. When meditating within the *jhanas,* the meditator is not disturbed by the neuroses of passion and aggression and is able to develop very clear and sharp insight into the nature of the mind. Of right samadhi, the Buddha said, "Any singleness of mind equipped with these seven factors—right view, right intention, right speech, right conduct, right livelihood, right effort, and right mindfulness—is called noble right concentration with its supports and requisite conditions."

Parting Thoughts

The Buddha was not trying to create a new religion with dogmas, priests, and rituals. His main concern was to give people a practical, workable system for self-discovery and spiritual advancement. He thought that his enlightenment, his awakening, was available to anyone willing to put in the hard work to achieve it.

His own approach was experimental, curious, and courageous. In fact, it was scientific; he performed experiments in the laboratory of his mind. He tried out the systems that were being taught in his day, tested their results for himself, and found them to be disappointing.

Nowadays we are in a position to do the same thing. We do not have to take the Buddha's teachings on blind faith. We can try them out for ourselves and see where they lead. That is exactly what he invited us to do.

After his awakening under the Bodhi tree, the Buddha had a long, forty-five-year career teaching and instructing disciples on the spiritual path. He guided a great many of them into the very same awakening that he himself had achieved. He established rules for his followers—monks, nuns, and laypeople—that would become the guidelines for the institutions that carried his tradition to the present day. Finally, at the age of eighty, his body succumbed to death and he entered *parinirvana*, the final nirvana after death. His final words to his disciples were an exhortation to exert themselves on the spiritual path: "All conditioned things are subject to decay; by striving earnestly, you will succeed in awakening."

Thank you so much
Diane Clarke

If you enjoyed this book, it would mean the world to me if you could leave me a review on Amazon as it lets other readers know this book is worth buying and really helps me reach more people.

Below Are Some Of My Other Books I'm Sure You Will Enjoy.

Yoga For Beginners: 45 Easy Poses To Relieve Stress, Lose Weight And Balance Your Mind

Meditation for Beginners: The Complete Guide To Meditation For Less Stress, Better Sleep, Increased Focus And Life Long Health

Mudras: 40 Powerful Hand Gestures To Unleash The Physical, Mental And Spiritual Healing Power In YOU!

Crystals: Crystal Healing For Beginners: How to Use the Power of Crystals to Balance Your Chakras, Improve Health, Cleanse Your Soul and Be Happy Everyday

Mindfulness: The Beginner's Guide to Living in the Moment to Achieve Less Stress, More Happiness & Inner Peace

Or you can visit me at
www.DianeClarkeZen.com

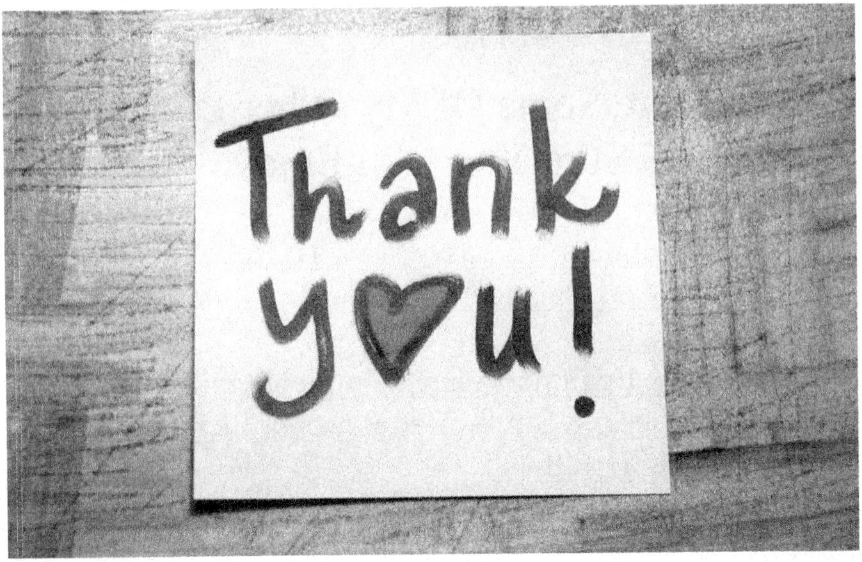
Thank you!

CPSIA information can be obtained
at www.ICGtesting.com
Printed in the USA
LVOW04s1339060616

491411LV00027B/543/P